# CORNISH TRACTION

## Stephen Heginbotham

AMBERLEY

I dedicate this book to my amazing eldest grandson, Callum, who has reached eighteen this year, against all the odds, and is a true spirit of inspiration, determination and unwavering happiness.

*Thanks to my wife, Julie, for her support while compiling this, my fourth book. Thanks also to Connor Stait of Amberley Publishing. Unless otherwise stated, all photographic content is courtesy of David Letcher or Ian Blackburn.*

First published 2018

Amberley Publishing
The Hill, Stroud
Gloucestershire, GL5 4EP

www.amberley-books.com

Copyright © Stephen Heginbotham, 2018

The right of Stephen Heginbotham to be identified
as the Author of this work has been asserted
in accordance with the Copyright, Designs and
Patents Act 1988.

ISBN 978 1 4456 7829 0 (print)
ISBN 978 1 4456 7830 6 (ebook)

British Library Cataloguing in Publication Data.
A catalogue record for this book is available from
the British Library.

Origination by Amberley Publishing.
Printed in the UK.

# Foreword

Following on from my successful previous books, I was invited by Amberley Publishing to compile a book featuring the various traction types in use in Cornwall over the recent decades.

This book features locomotives and other traction traversing the beautiful lines within Cornwall. Of course, as a former signalman and supervisor within Cornwall, I have encountered or signalled many of these locomotives, diesel multiple units (DMUs), HSTs and other trains countless times over almost a quarter of a century, prior to my retirement in 2015.

I was fortunate to be around when steam was still king on Britain's rail network and when trolleybuses and trams still traversed many of the country's cities and towns.

I feel privileged to have witnessed these transport treasures and my only regret is that I did not take more photographs, being armed only occasionally with the family Kodak Brownie, and in an age when film and processing was a prohibitive luxury that my pocket money would not support. It was only when I started work that there were any surplus funds for film, but not for a decent camera.

In a future book I will describe my career in signalling with the great British Railways, the not so great Railtrack and the far from great Network Rail.

Stephen Heginbotham

# Introduction

This book has been compiled using sets of photographs taken over several decades throughout Cornwall and depicts the many and varied traction types and trains that were once a familiar sight every day on the rails of the Duchy.

While Cornwall is generally associated with holiday trains, particularly serving idyllic locations such as St Ives and Newquay, it is often forgotten that freight played a substantial and important part in the development of the rail network. Indeed, large amounts of china clay are still carried within and beyond Cornwall, though sadly very little other freight is regularly moved by rail.

When I was a signalman at Lostwithiel and Par in the early 1990s, a record tonnage of over 1 million tons of china clay into Fowey Docks was achieved in a year. We still had the Postal trains, the fuel tanks were still delivering fuel to the depots at St Blazey and Penzance, and Fitzgerald Lighting wagons were delivered to and picked up from Bodmin Parkway.

Aside from the daily china clay traffic traversing the Fowey Branch, trains of high-quality clays were still being sent to Stoke-on-Trent and abroad, and the famous 'Silver Bullets' still ran up to Scotland with high-quality clay slurry.

In the periods covered in this book, there were Perishable, Milk, Newspapers and Parcels trains, as well as Holmans Engineering and other freight traffic. Where has all this freight gone? Well, on the roads mainly, and all because of political dogma and anti-rail policies.

Though such political short-sightedness has ostensibly disappeared in the main, there still remains a fragmented network driven by targets and subsidies, and the political dream of previous governments – that they could generate competition and improve things – has not happened, even though the various managements and politicians would have you believe otherwise.

As semaphore signals disappear throughout the country, here in Cornwall traditional signalling remains, and aside from minor upgrades soon to be installed, any transition to twenty-first-century technology is postponed for the foreseeable future.

The redoubtable Dr Richard Beeching and his report *The Reshaping of British Railways* were not the magic pill they were conceived as, all those years ago. Basically, he was an accountant and lacked the vision and foresight of the great innovators, engineers and pioneers that built the railways. Of course, nowadays he is reviled by many for destroying the network and for leaving many large and small communities without a decent public transport service. A good example is Tavistock, in West Devon, which is now trying to restore a rail link to Plymouth.

Many arguments about the Dawlish route have rumbled on for years, and it was certainly not the best of ideas to leave the West Country with just one extremely vulnerable route into the far west. Likewise, in Cornwall the route from Burngullow to Probus was singled in the 1980s, creating a logistical nightmare bottleneck and thus severely restricting any chance of a better train service and future growth. Fortunately, the double track was reinstated – at huge expense – in 2004, and the only restriction Cornwall has now is a lack of signals to improve the headway.

Cornwall, like many other rural areas, suffered at the hands of Dr Beeching and intransigent managements, but did manage to keep hold of some of its beautiful branch lines to the coast and country. The improvements on the Falmouth Branch in recent years have seen unprecedented growth in passenger numbers, and just go to prove that if you provide a decent service people will use it.

Cornwall has had a varied history of diesel traction types over the last six decades, after steam started to disappear in the 1960s. Like all things Great Western, the Western Region of British Railways was different when it came to diesel traction.

The main route out of London Paddington to the West Country and the ultimate destination of Penzance was once the domain of the diesel-hydraulics, such as the famous Westerns or Warships, and like the GWR previously, it wanted to promote its region by giving its frontline locomotives names that reflected both the region and its close association with the sea. These names meant something; they promoted the railway, and gave a sense of pride among the staff and people travelling along the Western Region routes.

The diesel-hydraulics were of course non-standard in British Railways terms, and as time went on it became apparent that these wonderful locomotives were on notice; as they came up for heavy overhaul, or as they failed, more and more were sidelined in favour of more standard locos, such as the ubiquitous Class 47s.

As the West Coast electrification was completed from London to Scotland, the English Electric locomotives that had been used north of Crewe became surplus and these were cascaded to the Western Region. So now the famous fifty – the Class 50s – started to replace the Westerns. The Western Region, of course, put their mark on them and they took the names of previously withdrawn locomotives, predominately with naval connections. By summer 1976, all fifty had been transferred, but the failure rate was high and availability down to 50 per cent at times, so they were progressively rebuilt/refurbished in the early 1980s. Though failures continued, reliability was much improved. By February 1987 spares were becoming scarce and BR seriously considered scrapping them all, but a traction shortage of suitable motive power prevented this. Consequently, No. 50011 was withdrawn as a source of spares and double-heading was used where possible to improve performance. More spares were needed so in July 1987 No. 50006 was withdrawn, followed by No. 50014 in December.

As we came through to the 1990s, the 50s slowly gave way to the HSTs, the Class 46s gave way to the 37s, and eventually, the Class 66s arrived for freight haulage. The Voyagers replaced the HSTs and Class 47s on cross-country workings, and while they are fast, they are noisy and uncomfortable in Standard Class – they are, after all, just DMUs! Soon we will see the next generation of passenger train replace the HST, which is, arguably, Britain's most successful train. As the modern railway tries to drag itself into the twenty-first century, we will soon see these new high-speed DMUs dominate the tracks. Aside from infrequent freight duties and occasional specials, the railways of the UK will be, in my opinion, a boring, corporate place for the true enthusiast.

The Class 47s were once the most prolific class of first generation diesel locomotive and were produced in large numbers during the 1960s. I liken their existence to the Stanier 'Black Five' steam locomotives of the former LMS and later BR, which were produced in equally large numbers and were general-purpose workhorses, which the trainspotters of the 1950s and 1960s sometimes ignored for the more exotic 'namers' that sped past or stood at the platform end with polished names and well-kept green or red paintwork.

Of course, the Class 47s had another claim to fame in that after the TOPS numbering system was introduced in the 1970s, some of them became the most renumbered locomotives ever seen on British railway metals, with some of them carrying up to six different numbers throughout their long existence. Previously, locomotives were rarely renumbered except for at Nationalisation.

In my trainspotting days, it was an exciting 'cop' if one of the four named Black Fives was seen because, until the run-down of steam started, they were rarely seen south of Carnforth, being predominately Scottish engines. However, at least one did migrate south permanently around 1964, and it was a true moment for me when, while journeying with Mum back home across Stockport one Saturday evening, standing on the middle road at Edgeley station was the celebrity loco No. 45154 *Lanarkshire Yeomanry*.

It's only when they start to disappear that people suddenly think that they need to take note of these 'workhorses' because one day, like the Black Fives, they will be gone – that is, except for the shiny preserved examples, pickled in aspic.

In 2018, the movement of freight within and from the Duchy is just a shadow of its former self, and even the ubiquitous CDA clay-carrying wagons have seen their numbers drastically reduced, while the sight of several locos, wagons and Royal Mail sets on St Blazey Depot have gone for ever. The previously bustling, busy depot is barely open, and most of the tracks are just rusting away, with tumbleweed blowing across the neglected yard. Penzance Depot, however, has seen a renaissance in recent years and is still a relatively busy place.

One thing is certain though – we will never see the likes of a Western, Warship, 37, 45, or 50 thrashing through the Duchy again, apart from the odd preserved example on a special.

I hope this collection of excellent photographs stirs memories of happier times on the tracks of the Royal Duchy. While most are of excellent quality, a few are not as good as one would have liked, but are included for their general interest and historical importance. Enjoy!

The last known Hymek working to Penzance. No. 7032 arrives at the terminus with a three-coach 'scratch' special working during an industrial dispute on Wednesday 19 April 1972. Hymeks were fairly uncommon visitors to Cornwall, and this one was withdrawn the following May after just eleven years of service. Designed for a thirty-year-plus service life, 101 were built by Beyer-Peacock in Gorton, Manchester, and most never even saw their first overhaul, some being withdrawn with only eight years of service!

Warship 824 *Highflyer* leaving Long Rock with an Up afternoon freight working on 3 September 1972. (D)824 was built in July 1960 by British Railways at Swindon and was one of the last three in service, being withdrawn in December 1972 and cut up at Swindon Works in June 1975. Twelve years of service for a locomotive was scandalously short, with some being less than ten years old when withdrawn. Of the seventy-one built, only two survive.

An atmospheric picture showing D1034 *Western Dragoon* and D1030 *Western Musketeer* at Platforms 2 and 3 respectively in Penzance station, 19 April 1972.

The Up Limited, with D1002 *Western Explorer* in charge, stands at Camborne station, as D1054 *Western Governor* approaches with the 23.55 Paddington to Penzance sleeper train, running 208 minutes late at 11.15 on 9 September 1972.

Original green-liveried Brush Type 4s Nos 1930 and 1745 are seen here stabled at Penzance station in September 1972. These locos suited their original livery well.

The 14.58 Penzance to Milton Keynes climbs towards Gwinear Road behind No. 47613 *North Star* on the same date. Of interest are the Mark III catering vehicle and two DVTs at the rear.

*Above*: Brush Type 4 No. 1679 and D1054 *Western Governor* on Long Rock Shed on 18 December 1972. No. 1679 would go on to become 47093 and lasted another nineteen years in service, unlike D1054, which had barely four years left.

*Right*: Here we see D1061 *Western Envoy* working a goods diagram. 6B30 propels a single 13-ton open wagon into Holmans Siding at Roskear Junction, Camborne, on 9 February 1973.

D1026 *Western Centurion* with 1E21, the Cornishman, passing the site of Carn Brea station (closed to passengers in 1961) on 27 February 1973.

Seen passing Carn Brea Yard Signal Box with five empty wagons for Holmans at Camborne at 10.17 on 27 February 1973 is D1017 *Western Warrior*, working freight diagram 6B19.

Brush Type 4s Nos 1664 *George Jackson Churchward* and 1668 *Orion* are seen here among the fuel tankers at Long Rock. The track in the foreground is positioned ready for re-modelling of the yard. No. 1664 survives as No. 57009 *Freightliner Venturer*. 13 March 1973.

On its way into Penzance station is No. *1664 George Jackson Churchward*, running light engine past Ponsandane Goods Shed to work 1A19, the Up Limited, on 13 March 1973.

Approaching St Erth is D1030 *Western Musketeer* with the 18.00 Penzance to Bristol train. Note the Up refuge siding still in situ, and 'Siphon G' on the back of the train. 10 April 1973.

A view from an Up train at Par station showing 'Bubble Car' No. W55016 and a Gloucester RCW three-car cross-country DMU stabled in the siding. 7 August 1973.

Seen at Bodmin Road and viewed from a Down train is Sulzer Type 2 No. 7574 with forty sheeted 13-ton china clay wagons bound for Fowey Docks on 7 August 1973.

*Right*: Lostwithiel station sees D1024
*Western Huntsman* working 6A21, an Up
Milk train, on 7 August 1973. Alas, the
old station buildings have long gone,
though a waiting room and shelter do
exist. Lostwithiel is in the bottom of the
valley and is virtually at sea level, so it
can flood, but requires hard acceleration
in both directions. The Up signal (LL5)
is the easiest to pull, being only a few
feet from the signal box, and the gantry
in the background with LL57 'off' controls
the freight branch to Fowey, LL54 being
the short arm to the left.

*Below*: Approaching Penponds Viaduct,
west of Camborne, is D1003 *Western
Pioneer* with a thirteen-coach Up empty
coaching stock (ECS) at 11.24
on 6 September 1973.

D1059 *Western Empire* and D1062 *Western Courier,* since preserved at the Severn Valley Railway (SVR), outside
Penzance station on 9 October 1973.

A work-stained Brush Type 4 still in green livery shunts stock away from Platform 3 at Penzance station on 9 October 1973. (D)1741 became No. 47148 and survived for another fourteen years in service.

*Above*: St Blazey turntable and semi-roundhouse with locomotives of Classes 46, 47 and 25 present on 16 April 1974.

*Left*: Camborne station sees D1067 *Western Druid* with 1A19, the Up Limited, on 25 May 1974.

A ten-coach Down passenger train (1B87), hauled by D1044 *Western Duchess* at 14.04, passes the site of the old Marazion station on 20 June 1974.

The Up IM74, the 14.00 Penzance to Birmingham, also passing the old Marazion station at 14.07 on 20 June 1974, is worked double-headed, with D1008 *Western Harrier* and D1053 *Western Patriarch* providing ample power.

Railman Bill Williams acting as flagman at Gwinear Road Level Crossing as No. 46004 and D1061 *Western Envoy* pass with the Up 1M74 Penzance to Birmingham on 1 July 1974.

The driver of D1044 *Western Duchess* talks to the signalman at Penzance while stood at signal PZ64 (the Section Signal to St Erth) at the old Marazion station with 1E21, the Up Cornishman, on 16 July 1974.

Ex-works D1006 *Western Stalwart* unusually enters Penzance station with 7B12, a Down morning freight working, on 19 July 1974. There was also a points failure near Ponsandane.

D1066 *Western Prefect* is seen leaving Penzance with 1E21, the Up Cornishman, and is about to pass the now preserved D1013 *Western Ranger* on Sea Sidings on 19 July 1974. Where the photographer is standing, and where D1013 is stood, is now the site of the coastal footpath/cycleway linking Penzance with Marazion.

The Down Cornishman running as 1V71, passing Hallenbeagle Mine engine house at Wheal Busy, Scorrier (east of Redruth), at 16.06 on Thursday 22 August 1974, hauled by No. 47064. One could not imagine a more typically Cornish scene!

D1023 *Western Fusilier* is seen passing over Hayle Viaduct with an Up train on 23 September 1974 (the author's twenty-third birthday). David Letcher's ex-GPO Morris 1000 van is parked on the station approach road. One of the piers of Hayle Viaduct close to the road leans by a few degrees and, in summer, when the visitors are down, we get occasional calls of alarm from people thinking it's falling over!

The twenty-three-wagon afternoon Up freight working approaches Trevingey Foot Crossing, Redruth, at 15.49 on Wednesday 19 March 1975 behind No. 25327.

On the Down line approaching Camborne station is No. 47239, which is hauling 1B25 at 09.30 on Thursday 27 March 1975. The driver is looking back at something towards the rear of the train.

An unidentified Class 47 powers through Camborne station with 4A13, the Up Perishables, which is loaded to twelve vehicles at 15.31 on Thursday 27 March 1975.

Passing the site of Onslow Siding, east of Bodmin Road, is No. 45040 *Kings Shropshire Light Infantry*, with 1M74, Penzance to Birmingham, at 15.24 on Monday 31 March 1975.

The St Austell to Kensington Olympia Motorail train is seen crossing West Largin Viaduct with eight passenger coaches and eleven bogie car flats at 16.30 on 31 March 1975, behind an unidentified Western. This view remains virtually unchanged today. A lonely spot in winter and at night, it is also reputed to be haunted!

An unidentified Peak with a Down passenger train (Load 8) is seen at 16.42, at the same location as the previous picture, on 31 March 1975.

*Above*: No. 46020 stands at Camborne station with 1M74 on a dismal Thursday 10 July 1975.

*Right*: Pausing at Redruth on the same date as the previous picture is No. 46002, with the 18.00 Penzance to Bristol.

Powering away from Truro is No. 47061 with the 08.00 Bristol to Penzance passenger train on Monday 11 August 1975. The industrial buildings opposite are on the site of the former Truro steam sheds.

Dropping down the hill and into Truro station is No. 47111 with the eight-coach Up 1M74 Penzance to Birmingham at 14.36 on Monday 27 October 1975.

With No. 46010 in charge, the ten-coach Up 1M74, Penzance to Birmingham, is waiting for departure time from Par at 15.11 on Wednesday 29 October 1975.

Climbing steadily towards Gwinear Road with the Up Perishables (4M05), and loaded to fifteen vans, is No. 47029. There are examples of vehicles from all four pre-Nationalisation companies within this train, as was quite often the case. Thursday 15 January 1976.

A minor derailment at St Erth on Saturday 17 January 1976; the rear wheel set of the grampus wagon has derailed. No. 46014 is in charge, displaying the Up Limited head code.

Single-line working was in place over the Down road, as witnessed by D1058 *Western Nobleman*, which was seen approaching with the Up Cornishman on Saturday 17 January 1976.

No. 47033 is seen with the 08.00 Bristol to Penzance, passing No. 46014 at St Erth on 17 January 1976.

On Penzance Shed on 2 May 1976 is D1048 *Western Lady*, which was another survivor into preservation, being withdrawn at the end of Western traction on the network in February 1977.

A very clean No. 47128, with the seven-coach Up 1M74 Penzance to Birmingham, is seen passing Dolcoath Milk Siding, near Camborne, at 14.24 on Wednesday 24 March 1976.

Work-stained No. 47060 accelerates from the Gwinear Road 'slack' (speed restriction) with the six-coach 09.30 Paddington to Penzance at 15.10 on Friday 26 March 1976.

No. P576, a Gloucester Railway Carriage & Wagon (RCW) three-car cross-country DMU, is seen entering Camborne station on an Up local working at 10.15 on Wednesday 21 April 1976.

An unidentified Class 46 moves away from St Dennis Junction towards Newquay with a train of track materials on a Sunday morning in April 1976.

No. 47113 with the Up Limited approaches Camborne, and is viewed here from the site of the former goods yard on Wednesday 21 April 1976.

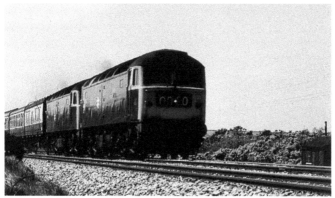

Double-headed Nos 47032 and 47185 with the ten-coach Up 1M74 Penzance to Birmingham are seen near Penponds Viaduct, west of Camborne, on Wednesday 28 April 1976.

The original Long Rock Shed at Penzance was still standing when this view of Nos 47512, 50002 and 47189 was taken on Sunday 2 May 1976.

Heading over Penponds Viaduct is No. 45049 *Staffordshire Regiment Prince of Wales' Own*, with a Saturday Penzance to Wolverhampton train (Load 11) at 09.59 on 26 June 1976.

A great photograph at Camborne station on Thursday 22 July 1976. No. 47112 is in charge of the Up Cornishman and D1033 *Western Trooper* is approaching the station on the Down with an ECS.

Despite the head code, this is No. 47119 at Penzance station shortly after arrival with the Down Limited on Monday 26 July 1976. This is a great photograph capturing holidaymakers and commuters arriving at this far-flung outpost of the former Great Western Railway.

'On the stopblocks' of Platforms 2 and 3 at Penzance are No 47119 and 47159. Both locos only ever carried these numbers. Monday 26 July 1976.

Dirty, green-liveried No. 47256 attracts the attention of a youthful admirer while waiting with the ten-coach Up Cornishman at Truro station at 11.01 on Tuesday 3 August 1976.

A view over the wall at Penzance station, portraying a care-worn No. 47088 *Samson* at Platform 2 on Saturday 14 August 1976. This was one of those locos that carried six different numbers through its life, being cut up as No. 47781 in 2007.

Another photograph of D1013 *Western Ranger*, this time on Penzance Shed on 14 August 1976. It had just six months left in service, but of course is still with us today.

D1068 and D1013 are seen on Penzance Shed, also on 14 August 1976. D1068 *Western Reliance* had just a few weeks left before withdrawal; she was cut up at Swindon a year later.

On the blocks of Platforms 2 and 3 at Penzance are Nos 50020 *Revenge* and 50006 *Neptune*. This idyllic scene was captured on Boxing Day 1976.

A picture included just to illustrate the shabby condition some locos were allowed to get into when they were approaching the end. On Boxing Day 1976 we see D1013 *Western Ranger* in Penzance station.

This great picture was taken on Boxing Day 1976 at Platform 1 at Penzance. Stabled are Nos 50035 *Ark Royal*, 47105, 47136, 50002 *Superb*, 47251 (now 57302) and 50042 *Triumph*. There is a very interesting fact attached to this photograph, in that every one of these six locos survives today!

Inside St Blazey Shed on Tuesday 28 December 1976 we find No. 46002. It is surprising how often it was possible to wander around this location without seeing a single railway employee!

Snow in Cornwall is something of a rarity. No. 45040 *Kings Shropshire Light Infantry,* with the eleven-coach afternoon Penzance to Birmingham train, is seen here crossing Brea Embankment adjacent to the site of North Crofty Junction on Wednesday 12 January 1977.

A view of No. 47089 *Amazon* on the Holmans Branch at Camborne, in the cramped confines of the yard and standing in what is now a part of Tesco's car park! The Holmans Branch was a junction just east of Roskear (Junction) Signal Box and served the heavy industry, which is long gone and is now the site of housing, supermarkets and other developments. Wednesday 9 February 1977.

Despite the head code, No. 45036 is leaving Par with 1M74, the afternoon Penzance to Birmingham train, while D1041 *Western Prince* stands in the loop alongside the Newquay platform with a short freight train. Note the smoke from the brake van chimney. Friday 11 February 1977.

Number 45059 (formerly D88) *Royal Engineer* stands at the blocks at Platform 2 in Penzance station after arrival with the Down Cornishman on Monday 21 February 1977.

The last Westerns were withdrawn on 27 February 1977, and D1013 *Western Ranger* was one of those to survive to the end. Seen here in Penzance station on 19 July 1974, she fortunately survived into preservation, and can normally be found on the Severn Valley Railway (SVR).

Here we see D1048 *Western Lady* in a rather unclear photograph on a very poor day for photography. The importance of the picture is in the fact that it is believed to be the very last time this loco worked this train (1M74), and possibly the last time it worked in Cornwall, being withdrawn within a day or so, in February 1977.

St Erth station sees No. 50022 *Anson* running light engine after being involved with permanent way engineering duties on 20 March 1977.

Standing inside the train shed at Penzance station, in Platform 1, on Monday 27 June 1977, we find No. 46054.

Just running into St Erth on Saturday 21 January 1978 with the Down Limited is No. 47513. In the dreaded leaf fall season, many trains struggle to depart from here towards Penzance due to leaves, the gradient and the curvature of the line. An automatic Sandite (sand/paste mixture) machine assists with traction during autumn.

A pair of Class 25s, Nos 25052 and 25080 (at the far end), heading towards St Blazey Yard from Par with a china clay train from the Parkandillack Branch on Tuesday 26 September 1978.

Heading towards St Blazey Yard with the afternoon freight from Penzance, No. 25207 passes the back of Par Signal Box on 26 September 1978.

Leaving Par with a train from Liverpool to Penzance is No. 50036 *Victorious*, seen on the afternoon of 26 September 1978. Signal PR 4 is still there today. The train has a short climb at 1 in 57 past Par Docks, then eases before a long 5-mile climb towards St Austell and Burngullow.

An HST power car from set 253001 is connected up to the mains in Ponsandane Yard at Penzance during the HST crew training period in Cornwall. Friday 3 November 1978.

Bodmin General station on Sunday 17 December 1978 sees two three-car Class 101 Diesel Multiple Units. DMUs B803 and 804 were used on a Lions Club sponsored 'Last trip to Wadebridge Rail Tour'.

Accelerating past Long Rock Depot and Ponsandane Sidings, which were temporary stabling sidings for the HST sets, is No. 50050 *Fearless* with the Up Midday Perishables on 3 November 1978. As D400, this was the first production locomotive of this class.

On New Year's Eve 1978, the Up Limited is hauled by No. 50017 *Royal Oak* and is seen here entering Camborne station.

Snow in Cornwall! No. 50017 *Royal Oak* is seen at Camborne station with the Up Limited on New Year's Eve 1978.

The Up Cornishman departing for Sheffield, from Camborne, on New Year's Eve 1978, with No. 50010 *Monarch*.

Entering Camborne station with an Up Parcels/Perishables train is No. 50039 *Implacable* on 2 January 1979.

On 14 March 1979, the afternoon Up Perishables was worked by Nos 50032 *Courageous* and 50010 *Monarch*, which are seen here in Camborne station. Interestingly, No. 50010 was the only one of the class broken up at Laira in May 1992, after nearly four years being stored as a source of spares.

A view from Pendarves Bridge, Camborne, of No. 46021 with the seven-coach Up Cornishman at 10.40 on Saturday 17 March 1979.

Seen here propelling its train from Hayle station onto the Wharves branch via the facing connection from the Up main line is No. 25225 on Tuesday 20 March 1979.

Shunting the Wharves Sidings at Hayle is No. 25225. Banana traffic was not a regular feature on this line; the vans were used as 'barrier vehicles' when tankers were conveyed. 20 March 1979.

An unidentified Peak passing Gwinear Road with the Up eight-coach 1M74 at 14.15 on Friday 23 March 1979. The gap in the Down platform marks the site of the former Gwinear Road West Signal Box.

A very early visit to Cornwall by Class 37s occurred on Saturday 14 April 1979, when Nos 37178 and 37084 worked the Pixieland Express from Worcester to Penzance. Here they are setting back from Platform 2 after the stock had been released by a Class 25 acting as station pilot. These were not exactly the cleanest locos, considering they were on railtour duties.

Penzance station Platforms 2 and 3 are hosting No. 50010 *Monarch* and the acting station pilot loco, No. 25058, on 14 April 1979.

Another trip freight to Hayle Wharves on Tuesday 19 June 1979 sees No. 25225, with the power station chimneys visible above the locomotive.

Viewed from St George's Walk, No. 25225 crosses from the Up main to the Down while leaving Hayle for Penzance with the return trip working on 19 June 1979.

Trevingey Footpath Crossing, near Redruth, sees No. 50026 *Indomitable* stood on the Up road with an engineers' permanent way train on 1 July 1979.

The Up Cornishman is seen passing over Redruth Viaduct 'Bang Road' during single-line working (SLW) with No. 50037 *Illustrious*. The adjacent line sees No. 50026 *Indomitable*, which is stationary with an engineers' train, on 1 July 1979.

It is Sunday 1 July 1979 and an unidentified Class 47 is seen passing over Dolcoath Level Crossing, and past the empty Dolcoath Milk Siding, near Camborne. The train of at least twelve coaches is running over the Down line (SLW) due to engineering work in the Redruth area.

Drump Road Goods Yard, Redruth, on Sunday 1 July 1979. A loco-spotter's dream sees No. 47111 about to regain the Up main line with an Up Milk/Van train, while Nos 50026 *Indomitable* and 46001 (numerically the first Class 46 and formerly D138) are engaged in permanent way duties.

Drump Road Goods Yard, Redruth, on Sunday 1 July 1979. Here we find Nos 50026 *Indomitable* and 46001 engaged in permanent way duties.

The crossover at Roskear Junction was still in regular use when No. 50028 *Tiger* backed its train for Paddington across it and onto the Down line on the afternoon of 1 July 1979. The pilotman will either accompany the train over the SLW section, or he could send it through if another train was following close behind it. He would then travel through with the second train. The crossover has now gone and the author was the last pilotman to accompany a train over it.

A view from the top deck of a Western National bus that the author had been driving at the time; with Carn Brea in the background, an unknown Class 47 powers away from Redruth station with a Down passenger working at 19.20 on Sunday 1 July 1979. The car park is well patronised with cars that would now be considered classics.

A nicely illuminated view at Redruth station of No. 47477, which is working the seven-coach 14.30 from Paddington to Penzance on Sunday 1 July 1979.

Waiting to depart Redruth is No. 47433, which is seen while working the 15.20 to Paddington on Thursday 5 July 1979. Formerly D1548, she was built in October 1963.

On 7 July 1979, an Up Paddington train with No. 50005 *Collingwood* in charge stands at Redruth waiting for the 'right away'. In the background is a Leyland National Series 1 bus belonging to Western National.

Passing the site of the former Gwinear Road station with a Down working for Penzance, at 10.42 on 14 July 1979, is No. 50009 *Conqueror*. The former branch line to Helston started from here.

A deserted Drump Road Goods Yard at Redruth with No. 46038 passing on the eight-coach Up 1M74, Penzance to Birmingham, on Monday 23 July 1979. National carriers' traffic had passed to road haulage by this time – an ignominious end for a once-busy railway goods yard. Note the signalman's Simca motor car parked opposite the box.

A low angle view of No. 45007 (D119) at Camborne station while working 1M74, the 13.56 Penzance to Birmingham, on Tuesday 24 July 1979.

The Up Cornishman (Load 12) is seen here at Camborne with No. 50039 *Implacable* on 19 August 1979.

Blasting away from Hayle and climbing towards Angarrack Viaduct with a lunchtime, Paddington-bound train on 20 August 1979 is No. 50025 *Invincible*.

A view looking back at the Royal Albert Bridge, Saltash, from an HST working the Down Limited on Thursday 11 October 1979.

An atmospheric picture of No. 47555 *The Commonwealth Spirit* inside the roundhouse at St Blazey on Thursday 10 January 1980. The Class 47 lasted another twenty years, but the roundhouse is still with us, though sadly devoid of locomotives.

Class 25 No. 25052 propels its train, under the watchful eye of the guard, towards the sidings at Hayle Wharves on Friday 22 February 1980.

Penzance driver Eddie Ralph is seen shunting in Hayle Wharves with No. 25052 on Friday 22 February 1980.

Detail of the 'aft end' of No. 45048 (D70) *The Royal Marines* while the loco has stopped at Camborne station with the 1M74 to Birmingham on Thursday 13 March 1980.

Shunting at Drump Road, Redruth, with empty cement wagons from Chacewater is No. 25080, on Friday 14 March 1980.

Redruth station is the setting for No. 46011, which is seen here with 1M74 on Saturday 22 March 1980, giving a clear view through the short tunnel at the Truro end of the station.

DMU set No. P463, with No. W51320 at the front, waits in the Newquay Branch platform at Par with a late-morning departure on Saturday 1 June 1980. The holidaymakers should have a more comfortable journey than in the second-generation DMUs used today.

Penzance station on Tuesday 4 June 1980. On the blocks in Platform 2 is power car No. W43140 (set No. 253035) and Bubble Car No. W55025 (with No. 55026) is in Platform 3.

With a Western National 'Cornish Fairways' bus, Series 1 Leyland National, fleet number 2815 (MOD 815P), in the background, No. 50046 *Ajax* waits at Redruth with an Up Perishables train, as No. 253019 emerges from the tunnel on the afternoon of Wednesday 25 June 1980.

The afternoon Up Perishables train is seen at Redruth station on 25 June 1980 with No. 50046 *Ajax*, and HST set No. 253019 on the Down.

No. 47476 stands with the Up empty diesel fuel tanks from Long Rock Depot, waiting for the signal to clear at Camborne station on Friday 15 July 1980.

Passing the entrance to the goods yard at St Austell is No. 37299, which is running 'light engine' in June 1982.

A few moments after the last picture was taken, No. 37142 passed on the Down with a train of sheeted clay wagons. The loco survived and is preserved on the Bodmin & Wenford Railway.

A pair of Bubble Cars, with Avon Link-branded No. 55033 leading, form a local Down service at Camborne station in July 1982. The Bubble Cars were a common sight, working in Devon and Cornwall for many years. Unlike the later single-unit Class 153s, the 121 and 122 Bubble Cars were purpose-built, first-generation DMUs.

A Saturday morning at Newquay station in July 1982. Three Class 47s with stock for Up country trains. The only one identified was No. 47076 *City of Truro*, whose driver is about to receive the single line token to St Dennis Junction from the signalman. It is hard to imagine now how Cornwall's principal tourist destination was downgraded to just a single platform!

Accidents do happen, although minor ones such as this were referred to as 'mishaps' by British Rail, and were usually quickly cleared up. How times have changed! No. 47125 is well and truly 'off the road' towards the east of Hayle station after making a wrong line move during an engineers' possession on a Sunday in July 1982. Single-line working was already in force and trains continued to pass the scene, albeit at a much-reduced speed! No. 47125 survived to be allocated number 47548, but it never carried it.

Heading along the causeway towards Tywardreath Highway in the summer of 1982 is No. 50042 *Triumph* with a train for Newquay. No. 50042 survived and is a resident loco on the Bodmin & Wenford Railway, here in Cornwall. This location is still the same today, with trains running along the causeway towards the 'section signal' (SB36) and thence 'up the hill' to Goonbarrow Junction, down the single line controlled by Electric Token.

An Up air-braked, long-distance freight service comes around the sharp curve from St Blazey into Par station behind an unidentified Class 47 on Monday 21 March 1983. This scene is virtually unchanged today.

No. P460, a three-car DMU, enters the Down platform at Par station to form an afternoon local working to Penzance on Monday 21 March 1983.

A two-car DMU, No. P480, waits at the south Cornish coastal terminus at Looe on Tuesday 22 March 1983.

A view from Liskeard Signal Box as No. 50029 *Renown* comes off the viaduct towards the station with a Down afternoon express passenger working on Tuesday 22 March 1983. The only thing missing from this picture today would be the Up gantry signals. The main arm and shunting signal (LD4 and 5) were taken away when St Germans Signal Box was removed in the late 1990s. They were replaced by a colour light on the far end of the viaduct (LD4). Liskeard Signal Box now works to Plymouth Panel in the Up direction and Lostwithiel in the Down.

In happier times, before the over-rationalisation, we find No. 50012 *Benbow* at Newquay station on Saturday 30 July 1983.

Entering Newquay with an overnight holiday train is No. 50019 *Ramillies*, as sister loco No. 50012 *Benbow* waits in the platform on 30 July 1983.

Nos 50012 *Benbow* and 50019 *Ramillies* at Newquay station on 30 July 1983. No. 50019 appears to be in the process of running around and No. 50012 has cleared out of the way.

An unidentified Class 50 with an Up Motorail train from St Austell threads through the golf course at Carlyon Bay on Saturday 13 August 1983. The cars parked near the loco are at an access point gate, which the author had renamed Renshaw's Gate a few years ago in memory of a former railwayman and colleague of mine who had passed away at an early age and while on duty.

In August 1983 at Lostwithiel we see No. 37270 'running round' its train, which will be in the Down loop behind it. The train will have traversed the branch line from Fowey Docks, and will probably consist of up to nineteen CDA type wagons, which will now return to either Goonbarrow or Burngullow to be refilled. (Graham Pearse)

St Erth station with an unidentified Class 45/46 running in on the Down line with a passenger train in August 1983. (Graham Pearse)

Officers' Inspection Saloon KDW No. 150266, seen here being hauled by No. 50004 *St Vincent*, is passing Gwinear Road on Thursday 20 October 1983. You always had a clean loco if it was on an 'Officers Special' duty.

An unidentified Class 50 passes St Germans Signal Box with a Down train of CDA wagons full of china clay, bound for Fowey Docks. I say 'signal box', but it was actually the old Up waiting room, which was equipped with a temporary rudimentary panel after the real box was demolished. This 'temporary' arrangement lasted twenty-five years! (Ian Blackburn)

Class 37 No. 37196 *Tre-Pol & Pen* rounds the curve from St Blazey into Par through siding with a Goonbarrow Junction–Fowey china clay train on 30 August 1985. (Ian Blackburn)

Another picture of No. 37196, this time taking the Drinnick Mill portion of the Dover–St Blazey Polybulks away from Par, seen on the same date as the previous picture. (Ian Blackburn)

About to tackle the bank out of Par on 1C48, Paddington–Penzance, on 30 August 1985 is No. 50050 *Fearless*. Originally numbered D400, this was the first of the fifty 50s built at the English Electric Vulcan Works, and it entered service in October 1967 at Crewe. (Ian Blackburn)

Roaring through Liskeard station on the Up line is No. 47407 *Aycliffe*, which is at the head of 3S15, a Penzance–Cardiff Parcels train, on 18 October 1985. Built in January 1963, she was withdrawn five years after this photograph was taken, and stored for a further five years before being scrapped in December 1995. (Ian Blackburn)

Here we have No. 37185 at Newquay with a train of Turbot wagons on Sunday 5 February 1984, complete with Cornish Railways logo.

Stabled in Penzance station on 14 February 1988 are Nos 50046 *Ajax* and 50040 *Centurion*. The latter had been previously named *Leviathan*, only losing this name a few months before this picture was taken.

Platform 3 at Penzance finds Network SouthEast-liveried No 50018 *Resolution* at the head of an Up passenger working in March 1988. The '50s lent themselves well to both large logo and NWSE liveries.

On 21 May 1988, Penzance station was host to (from left to right): Nos 50038 *Formidable*, 50036 *Victorious*, 47629 (survived), 47591 (survived), 47639 *Industry Year 1986* (survived) and 47544, which is seen at the head of the 10.17 to Manchester.

Class 37 No. 37675 *William Cookworthy* draws 6B74, the 06.45 Par–Drinnick Mill empty 'Dustbins', out of Par Down Goods Loop on the cold and misty morning of Wednesday 22 June 1988. (Ian Blackburn)

The driver of Plymouth set No. 872 exchanges tokens with the signalman at Goonbarrow Junction *c.* 1988. This is a mixed set comprising of half a 101 and what appears to be half a Class 108 unit. These first-generation units were often found in unusual formations towards the end of their working lives. (Ian Blackburn)

Cornish DMUs; Sprinter set No. 155323 arrives at Liskeard station on 2C85, the 15.35 Penzance–Plymouth working, *c.* 1988. Destined to become two 153 units, they are still in daily use thirty years later. Of particular interest here is LD3, which is the only remaining wooden somersault signal still in use on the Western Route. (Ian Blackburn)

An unidentified Class 47 is seen here in the Up direction, passing through Largin with an express freight *c.* 1988. The isolated former signal box at Largin was the control location for regulating the single line over both of the viaducts and was a signalman's dream location, being more akin to somewhere like Blea Moor on the Settle–Carlisle line. (Ian Blackburn)

Out of the sunlight and into the shade at Largin as 1C32, the 10.50 Paddington–Penzance, winds its way through the woods on 1 March 1988. It is about to pass the famous Largin Signal Box. (Ian Blackburn)

An HST in the earlier livery passes Largin Signal Box in the Up direction *c.* 1988. (Ian Blackburn)

HST set No. 253025 in the early livery passes over Largin Viaduct with a Down train *c.* 1988. (Ian Blackburn)

HST set No. 253045 is seen here on the Up line passing Roskear Junction Signal Box *c.* 1988. (Ian Blackburn)

Another HST set, but with no visible identification, is about to pass Roskear Signal Box on the Up line. (Ian Blackburn)

An unidentified Class 45 passes over the Largin single line with an Up Parcels train *c.* 1988. (Ian Blackburn)

Large logo No. 47526 *Northumbria* stabled at Penzance station on Sunday 2 April 1989. One of the last to be built, as D1109 in January 1967, she is shown as now being with West Coast Railway Company at Carnforth.

InterCity-liveried No. 47508 *SS Great Britain*, with very small numerals, is also stabled at Penzance station on 2 April 1989. Built in October 1966, it was one of the last built, and was the first 47 to carry this name, giving it up in 1992 just before its early withdrawal.

Network SouthEast livery lends itself well to No. 50026 *Indomitable*, which is seen here in Platform 3 at Penzance station on 2 April 1989.

An unusual motive power combination at the head of the Up Royal Mail train at Penzance on Friday 14 April 1989 sees No. 47558 *Mayflower* piloted by No. 37675 *William Cookworthy* – a Cornish loco for many years and more usually found at the head of a train of wagons carrying china clay.

Viewed from the then accessible A30 road embankment, No. 47626 *Atlas* crosses the Hayle River shortly after leaving St Erth with an Up Van train at 12.25 on Friday 28 April 89.

Approaching Grampound Road in June 1989 is celebrity Class 47 locomotive No. 47500 *Great Western*, wearing Brunswick Green livery. This loco survives today. (Graham Pearse)

In June 1989 we see an unidentified Class 47 passing the site of the former Grampound Road station, which clearly shows the single-line section between Burngullow and Probus. This long section was re-doubled in 2004. (Graham Pearse)

Large logo-liveried No. 47816 and DVT No. 82114 pass the site of the former Gwinear Road station with the twelve-coach SO Milton Keynes to Penzance at 13.42 on 15 July 1989. The line falls away for over 4 miles now towards Hayle and St Erth, over the Angarrack Viaduct, and 65 mph will be easily achieved.

Class 108 diesel multiple units Nos 828 (three cars) and 957 (two cars) arrive at and leave St Erth with a Penzance to St Ives working at 11.17 on Saturday 5 August 1989.

Standing in Platform 4 at Penzance station is No. 47648 with the stock for the SO Penzance to Glasgow sleeper service on 5 August 1989. Renumbered to 47850 a few months later, she gave another six years of service.

On the same date as the last picture we find Platform 2 occupied by No. 47705 in the revised Network SouthEast livery at the head of an engineering train, with a former GWR 'Toad' brake van in its formation. In the background, seen in the yard, are a Bubble Car unit, a Class 108 unit and a Class 08 shunter, along with the stock for the Glasgow sleeper service on Platform 4.

*Above and below*: Long Rock Depot is host to No. 50024 *Vanguard* on Saturday 5 August 1989.

Another large logo-liveried loco, No. 47551, with a Penzance to Manchester passenger train, is at at Camborne station on Saturday 12 August 1989.

InterCity-liveried No. 47804 *Kettering*, with DVT No. 82120 at the rear, pass the site of the former Carn Brea station with the SO Milton Keynes–Penzance at 13.44 on Saturday 12 August 1989.

Departing St Erth with the 14.58 SO Penzance to Milton Keynes on 12 August 1989 is No. 47603 *County of Somerset*, with DVT No. 82120 as the first vehicle behind the loco. Most of the infrastructure at St Erth appears the same today, but the Down sidings are disconnected and the east end cross-over has been removed. The train will run downhill to Hayle Causeway then climb for 4 miles at a ruling gradient of 1 in 61.

Crossing Angarrack Viaduct from Penzance, on Saturday afternoon 12 August 1989, is an Up Van train headed by No. 37672 *Freight Transport Association*.

*Above*: Large logo No. 47806 approaches Camborne station with a Penzance to York passenger train at 11.12 on Saturday 12 August 1989. The gradient up to Camborne station is as steep as 1 in 55 in places.

*Right*: Bodmin Parkway station sees Nos 37674 and 37671 *Tre-Pol & Pen* shatter the peace as they pass through with an Up freight train at 16.58 on 18 August 1989.

*Above*: The Down Glasgow to
Penzance train, formed of HST set
No. 253037, enters Bodmin Parkway
at 17.02 on Friday 18 August 1989.

*Left*: Passing HSTs at the west end
of Truro station; power car No. 43137
is at the rear of a service from Bristol
as the 15.45 Penzance to Paddington
arrives on the Up at 16.21 on
19 August 1989.

Unfortunately, this is not a sight we are ever likely to witness again! Much noise heralded the approach of No. 37674, which was working hard through Penwithers Junction with a poorly HST set from Paddington, comprising Nos 43163 and 43138, and running very late on 19 August 1989. In the days of a joined-up railway, organising assistance was not the political game of charades it is now.

In the words of the singer/songwriter Mary Hopkins, 'Those were the days' – and indeed they were! No. 37674 is seen again with the ailing HST set, comprising Nos 43138 and 43163, but is now only fifteen minutes late with the return working, the 16.20 Penzance to Paddington, arriving in Truro. I can imagine that the departure from Truro would be in the best tradition of a good 37 with a Snake Pit driver on the 'big handle'.

Bearing a unique LNER-inspired apple-green livery is No. 47522 *Doncaster Enterprise*. The location is Penwithers Junction, Truro, with the afternoon Van train at 14.55 on Saturday 19 August 1989.

Network SouthEast-liveried No. 47573 *The London Evening Standard* is seen passing Penwithers Junction with the 08.45 Paddington to Penzance on Saturday 19 August 1989. The line to Falmouth diverges from the main line here and this former, once-busy signal box controlled the junction and the junction to Newham Wharf.

Celebrity loco No. 47500 *Great Western* runs past Penwithers Junction towards Truro with the 14.58 SO Penzance to Milton Keynes at 15.31 on 19 August 1989.

The Up Limited entering Camborne station on an unrecorded date, and wearing the first of the 'privatised liveries', which, being white on the lower portions, soon got very work stained and was hard to keep clean.

Large logo No. 47585 *County of Cambridgeshire* and No. 08576 share Platform 3 at Penzance station on Monday 12 March 1990. Built as D1779 in 1964, her final number was 47757, and she was cut up in 2006 after two years of storage.

Platform 4 at Penzance station is host to No. 47468 with an Up Van train on Monday 16 July 1990.

Running into Redruth station at 10.30 on 25 July 1990, with the Down Postal/Parcels train, is an unidentified large logo-livered Class 47. (Graham Pearse)

A Penzance panorama on Wednesday 8 September 1990 featuring, from left to right, Nos 47468, 08801, 47465 and 47801. Halcyon days!

Class 47 No. 47971 *Robin Hood* was built as D1616 in September 1964, but was renumbered 47037 in March 1974. It then became No. 97480 in September 1988 while carrying experimental equipment, but was allocated its final number in July 1989. It is seen here on the Up line passing Roskear Junction Signal Box with a Parcels train *circa* 1990. (Ian Blackburn)

# About the Author

I was born in 1951 and raised in Stockport, Cheshire, and after working for The National Bus Company for many years, I joined British Railways as a signalman at Furness Vale in Derbyshire, transferring to Lostwithiel, Cornwall, in 1992. In 1994, with the creation of Railtrack, I was promoted to Signalling Inspector in Cornwall, joining the Operations Team at St Blazey, where I worked as a Mobile Operations Manager (MOM) in the Old Station House, which was the one-time GWR ticket office for the long defunct St Blazey station.

Under Network Rail the job title changed to MOM, and a move around the corner to Par came in 2014. I then had an accident late in 2013 while alighting a loco in Penzance during a severe storm; this led to a desk job until I retired in 2015.

I have had a lifelong interest in all things transport, including studying for many years the railway accidents and incidents that have led to the signalling systems and rules we use today.

I have been very fortunate to work in an industry that is both my hobby and my career, and for the most part it has been an absolute pleasure to go to work every day, even though that meant thirty-six years of unsociable shifts, early starts and late finishes. I do, however, feel that changes in recent years within the industry have fragmented the 'big family' that was once BR.

Born in an age of steam, I well remember the transition from steam to diesel and electric, and was fortunate enough to see steam to its demise in August 1968, Stockport Edgeley (9B) being one of the very last steam sheds. As a child I watched named trains, with named locos, thunder past my school, and at weekends or school holidays I watched the Woodhead Electrics at Reddish, the trolleybuses in Manchester, or Pacifics on the West Coast or Crewe, making the journey there by either steam train or pre-war bus.

Once a year there was a family holiday in Blackpool, which meant passing the engine sheds at Preston and at other locations along the route through Lancashire, and spending many hours watching the trams both along the promenade or at the depot, where I was allowed to roam freely.

I was a member of the preservation movement for many years from the mid-1960s and was actively involved in helping to save some important vehicles for our heritage.

## Dave Letcher

I obtained my first 35 mm camera in 1969 and have been a keen photographer ever since. I continued to take railway photographs throughout the intervening years and amassed a huge collection of colour slides before making the change to digital. Most of my images in this volume have been scanned from those slides, some taken with quite primitive cameras and often, regrettably, on cheap film.

I was born in 1951 within earshot of the old Great Western Railway main line through Cornwall, not far from Carn Brea station, and I have been interested in railways for as long as I can remember. Among my earliest railway memories are visiting the goods yard there with my father, as he unloaded coal wagons onto my uncle's Bedford lorry. Here also I was acquainted with pannier tank locomotives Nos 3702 and 9748 of Truro and Penzance sheds, respectively, along with 2-6-2 tank No. 4554. Footplate rides around the yards at Carn Brea were partaken with relish, along with visits to Carn Brea Signal Box. An invite onto the footplate of No. 1018 *County of Leicester* as the loco stood in Platform 3 of Penzance station was a particularly fond memory.

My interest in railways continued unabated and I remember being particularly unimpressed with the new diesels as they began to appear at the end of the 1950s. Once, a very proud driver of D800 *Sir Brian Robertson*, in Penzance station with the Up Mail, showed me his cabs and engine room and asked what I thought of it. I said I preferred the Grange Class loco that was at the adjacent platform.

As a thirteen-year-old, I got to know a signalman at Gwinear Road West Signal Box and I became proficient at operating the frame and block instruments while he, along with the local shunter and the crew of the Up evening goods train, played cards in the brake van. The only thing that I wasn't allowed to do was to write anything in the train register!

As steam traction disappeared from the Cornish main line, excursions further afield became necessary to find working steam locomotives. These were undertaken whenever funds allowed.

In the late 1970s and early 1980s, I made numerous trips to various locations around the UK in pursuit of industrial steam, which was something that I had been largely dismissive of while there was still steam traction on the national network. In 1970, I became involved with the Great Western Society at Bodmin General station, and subsequently with the Cornish Steam Locomotive Preservation Society. When the signalling system was installed at Bodmin General, I registered my interest in training to become a signalman there and was duly trained and passed out as competent by the Signalling Inspector, Stephen Heginbotham, in June 2012. I still love working in that capacity as a volunteer.

## Ian Blackburn

Ian Joined BR at Kensington (Olympia) in 1973, becoming a signalman at Kensington, Chelsea and Latchmere Junction in 1973, before moving to Cornwall in 1974. He became a signalman at St Blazey in February 1975, and then at Par in July 1977.

Ian was promoted to Relief Signalman, covering all Cornish boxes and crossings until redundancy came in 1993, following which he then set up Amethyst Photography and Caversham Studios. Ian returned to the railway in 1998 to fund his daughter's education as a signalman at Roskear Junction. In May 2001 he took up a signalman's position at Stourton, near Leeds, and thence to York IECC Signalling Centre as a signalman in January 2002, later becoming Signal Box Manager there in 2004. He retired from the railway due to reorganisation.

Ian can now be found operating his garden railway, Consolidated Shales Heavy-Haul Railway, in North Wales.

## Reference Sources

Marsden, Colin J., *The Complete UK Modern Traction Locomotive Directory* (2011).
Allen, Ian, *BR Main Line Gradient Profiles* (1997).
Notes supplied by D. Letcher, I. Blackburn and G. Pearse.
My own contemporaneous notes and archive records.